Expressionism Art Kit

Artists in Profile

EXPRESSIONISTS

Merilyn Holme & Bridget McKenzie

Heinemann Library
Chicago, Illinois

Customer Service 888-454-2279
Visit our website at www.heinemannlibrary.com

Designed by Tinstar Design
Originated by Ambassador Litho
Printed by South China Printing Company, China

Library of Congress Cataloging-in-Publication Data
Holme, Merilyn, 1946-
  Expressionists / Merilyn Holme, Bridget McKenzie.
    p. cm. -- (Artists in profile)
Includes bibliographical references and index.
Summary: Discusses the characteristics of the Expressionism movement
which flourished in Germany from 1905 to 1920 and presents biographies
of fourteen Expressionist artists.
  ISBN 1-58810-647-0
  1. Expressionism (Art)--Juvenile literature. 2. Expressionism
(Art)--Germany--Juvenile literature. [1. Expressionism (Art) 2.
Artists.] I. McKenzie, Bridget, 1967- II. Title. III. Series.
  N6494.E9 H65 2002
  759.06'42--dc21
                            2001005436

Acknowledgments
The publisher would like to thank the following for permission to reproduce photographs: p. 4 DACS 2002/Paul Klee Foundation, Bern, Switzerland/Bridgeman Art Library; pp. 7, 12, 18 DACS 2002/Tate, London 2002; p. 9 DACS 2002/E. Lessing/SMPK Nationalgalerie, Berlin/AKG London; p. 10 DACS 2002/Busch-Reisinger Museum, Cambridge Mass.; p. 15 DACS 2002/Menard Art Museum, Aichi, Japan/AKG London; pp. 17, 27, 33, 38, 47, 50 AKG London; p. 20 Germanisches Nationalmuseum, Nurnberg; p. 22 Museum Ludwig, Cologne/AKG London; p. 25 DACS 2002/Paul Klee Stiftung Kunstmuseum, Bern; p. 29 DACS 2002/Stedelijk Van Abbe Museum, Eindhoven/AKG London; p. 31 E. Lessing/AKG London; p. 35 DACS 2002/AKG London; p. 36 Westfalisches Landesmuseum, Munster/AKG London; p. 37 Neue Pinakothek Munich/Artothek; p. 39 Stadt Galerie im Lenbachhaus, Munich/AKG London; p. 40 Museum Folkwang, Essen; p. 43 Munch Museum, Oslo; p. 45 DACS 2002/Photo Scala, Florence; p. 49 ©Nolde–Stiftung Seebull; p. 51 Sprengel Museum, Hannover; p. 53 Historisches Museum der Stadt, Vienna, Austria/Bridgeman Art Library; p. 54 DACS 2002/Peggy Guggenheim Collection, Venice/Cameraphoto/AKG London.

Cover photograph by Nolde-Stiftung Seebull/AKG.

Every effort has been made to contact copyright holders of any material reproduced in this book. Any omissions will be rectified in subsequent printings if notice is given to the publisher.

Some words are shown in bold, **like this.** You can find out what they mean by looking in the glossary.

Contents

What Is Expressionism?

Expressionism is an art movement that produced modern and colorful works of art. The lives of the artists who created these works were no less colorful and exciting. The word *expressionism* can be used to describe art from different times and places but most of the Expressionist artists in this book were part of a movement that took place in Germany from 1905 to 1920. Other artists have been included because they influenced those German Expressionist artists or they shared some of their beliefs. They believed that art should try to change society, to make it less **conservative.** It should express the energy of nature— following in the footsteps of Vincent van Gogh—and express personal feeling rather than simply represent nature. It should feel uncomfortable, which means it should challenge the traditional ways of looking at the world. Expressionist art should be inspired by folk art and the art of what were then called **primitive** peoples, such as those from Africa.

A Plan of Garden Architecture, by Paul Klee (1920)
The goal of the Expressionists was to express personal feelings about what they were painting rather than to represent it exactly as it was.

It should have strong colors and shapes, be relatively direct and unplanned, and still contain recognizable things without appearing realistic. The lines could be distorted and the colors could be strengthened or changed, as in Fauvism, an art movement that began in 1905 in France.

Expressionism was more than a style of painting. It could be found in theater and movies, literature, and architecture. It was a sharing of ideas and experiences across all these media. The life stories of the Expressionist artists show just how much they had in common. Many began by studying **applied art,** such as furniture design, often to please their parents. Although they later made more personal art, they continued to make use of those technical skills. Both art critics and the public received this new movement with surprise and outrage. Expressionist artists were trying to shock by challenging the traditional, conservative views held by many people. Gradually, however, Expressionist art became accepted and even admired.

All of the Expressionists were affected by World War I (1914–1918). Some fled from Germany and spent the war years in exile. Some never returned to their homeland. Most served in the war, and some were killed. At first some of them hoped war would change society for the better, but they were soon disillusioned when they saw the destruction and suffering that it caused. In the years after the war, many Expressionist artists revealed the horrors they experienced in their work.

After World War I, Expressionism became very fashionable in Germany, where art was allowed to flourish. This freedom ended in 1933 when Hitler declared all Expressionists were **degenerate.** This led to them being fired from their jobs or forced to leave Germany. In 1937, the Nazis took thousands of pieces of art from German museums and put them in an enormous exhibition called the Degenerate Art Exhibition. They wanted to show how bad and **decadent** this art was. It presented a view of the world that went against their political and cultural ambitions of ridding Germany of all inferior races.

Vincent van Gogh (1853–1890)

The German Expressionists and the French **Fauves** were both influenced by the paintings of Vincent van Gogh, who presented a highly personal view of nature. He used vivid colors and exaggerated, swirling brush strokes to give a sense of energy and movement to everything he portrayed. He said, "Instead of trying to reproduce exactly what I have before my eyes, I use color more arbitrarily [in an unplanned way] so as to express myself more forcibly." This Dutch artist moved to Arles in the south of France in 1888. He was inspired by the bright colors there, and by the way the light appeared. He painted over two hundred pictures in the two years he lived in Arles, before he died in 1890.

Fauvism and Matisse

An exhibition in 1905 at the fall **Salon** in Paris kicked off the first **avant-garde** art movement of the twentieth century. The colors of the paintings by Matisse, Derain, and Maurice de Vlaminck shown in this exhibition were more vivid and unrealistic than had ever been seen before. The artists were labeled *Fauves,* or wild beasts. They were a big influence on the German Expressionists.

Henri Matisse (1869–1954) was one of the *Fauves.* He wrote, "What I dream of is an art of balance, of purity and serenity . . . like a comforting influence, a mental balm—something like a good armchair." His belief that art should be comfortable differed from the Expressionists, who believed that art should express one's true feelings, however ugly and violent they may sometimes be.

The Nazis disliked Expressionist artists because many lived in an unconventional, **bohemian** way. These artists did not often settle in their home towns, because they needed to search for like-minded artists and new ideas for their art. They traveled outside their countries to see other artists' work, as good color reproductions were not available. In particular, they wanted to visit France to see art by van Gogh, André Derain, Matisse, and Robert Delaunay, whom they especially admired. They were also keen to meet artists and thinkers from other countries. A large number taught in art schools and were intellectuals and writers. Expressionism was about more than personal emotion. Most Expressionists were active members of artist groups. They wanted to display their art together and make public, sometimes shocking, statements about their beliefs.

Although a great deal was shared, above all, Expressionism was about the strength of the individual. Through their art, the Expressionists stated that emotions matter and should not be repressed, and that our feelings distort our vision, making us all see the world in unique ways.

Die Brücke

Brücke means bridge in German. The name suggests that this group wanted to make a path to the future. They also wanted to make a bridge between fine art and design. They were driven by the ideas of Ernst Kirchner, who with Fritz Bleyl, Erich Heckel, and Karl Schmidt-Rottluff, formed the group in 1905. At the time, the artists were all architecture students interested in painting. They believed that artists should feel free to express themselves in a way that comes naturally to them, unrestricted by traditional, established values and styles.

▮▮▮ *Male Head,* by Karl Schmidt-Rottluff (1917)
Schmidt-Rottluff, a former architecture student, was a founding member
of Die Brücke. *He introduced Emil Nolde to the group.*

A statement of 1906 says, "We believe in development and in a generation of people who are both creative and appreciative; we call together all young people, and—as young people who bear the future—we want to acquire freedom for our hands and lives, against the well-established older forces."

Common themes of *Die Brücke* paintings are people and unspoiled nature. But their painting style, compared to *Der Blaue Reiter* artists, could be harsh, with angular figures; colors that combined clashing, acid brights with moody darks; and nervous brush strokes. Some say that their style was so rough because they had not been trained to paint. Others say that it was the result of the direct expression of emotion. In addition to painting, they made a lot of woodcut prints. They thought this old German art form was well-suited to the expression of feelings because of its strong black and white contrasts. They made many copies of their prints so that as many people as possible could see and own their work.

Der Blaue Reiter

Der Blaue Reiter is German for "The Blue Rider." It was not the name of a fixed group of artists, but of a magazine, or almanac, containing writings about art, music, and theater. It was illustrated with folk art, medieval art, and Egyptian art, and drawings by children and **Fauve** and Expressionist artists. Wassily Kandinsky produced this almanac in 1912 with Paul Klee, Franz Marc, August Macke, Gabriele Münter, and Alexei von Jawlensky. All the artists involved in *Der Blaue Reiter* were located in or near Munich, Germany. They had an interest in freeing the picture from the object. In other words, they believed that art did not have to mirror actual appearances. Their art was very colorful and was often **abstract,** especially in Kandinsky's case. They were influenced by both German and Russian folk art. They liked its stories and its simple woodcut styles and flat compositions.

The Bauhaus

Many Expressionist artists later were involved with the Bauhaus. The Bauhaus was a school of design, and a center for **Modernism.** It was set up in 1919 by Walter Gropius. Like the *Brücke* artists, he wanted to mix fine art with design. So, many of the Bauhaus teachers were painters, including Kandinsky and Klee. They worked hard to give the architecture and design students a more sensitive awareness of color and form. The typical Bauhaus design style is very geometrical and simple, and not very Expressionist. The school changed cities three times and was finally closed by the Nazis in 1933.

■■ *The Almanac,* Der Blaue Reiter, Wassily Kandinsky (1912)
The almanac was edited by Kandinsky and Marc and included contributions by both Expressionist and Fauvist artists. In 1930, Kandinsky wrote: "We invented the name 'Der Blaue Reiter' while sitting at a coffee table in the garden in Sindelsdorf; we both loved blue, Marc liked horses, I riders. So the name came by itself."

Max Beckmann (1884–1950)

- Born February 12, 1884 in Leipzig, Germany
- Died December 27, 1950 in New York

Key works

The Self-Portrait with a Red Scarf, 1917
The Night, 1918–1919
The Synagogue, 1919
Carnival, 1920
Before the Masked Ball, 1922
Departure, 1932–1935

Self-Portrait with Dinner-Suit, ⎮
Max Beckmann (1927)
"*What I want to show in
my work is the idea which
hides itself behind so-calle
reality. I am seeking for th
bridge which leads from
the visible to the invisible
. . .*" (Max Beckmann,
speaking of his work
in 1938.)

Max Beckmann was born in 1884, the third child of a wholesale flour merchant. The family lived in Leipzig until Beckmann's father died in 1894. Then they moved to Braunschweig. Here, Beckmann went to school. He started to draw at the age of five and neglected his schoolwork in favor of this activity. Finally, only fifteen years old, his mother allowed him to leave school and go to the Weimar Academy of Art. He stayed there for three years and gained a solid training in painting people. In 1903, he visited Paris. In 1904, he won a prize to study for six months in Florence, Italy, where he could visit churches to see early religious art. He became interested in how pictures could tell stories in passionate but clear ways. In 1905, he moved to Berlin, which was the cultural and administrative center of Germany.

Beckmann's first paintings reflected his respect for the Impressionist and Post-Impressionist paintings he had seen in Paris. In 1906 he was awarded a prize for his picture *Young Men by the Sea* by the German Artists' League at Weimar. That same year he joined a group of artists known as the Berlin **Secession,** and he married Minna Tube, a fellow artist whom he had met at the Weimar Academy. He turned again to early French and Dutch painting and chose mostly biblical and mythical scenes as subjects for his pictures.

However, this changed after World War I. In 1914, Beckmann volunteered for the medical corps, which meant that he had to help badly wounded soldiers. This experience led to a nervous breakdown in 1915. He was discharged from the army to a hospital in Frankfurt.

Otto Dix (1891–1969)

Otto Dix, Beckmann, and George Grosz were the main artists of the **New Objectivity** movement of the 1920s, which was a reaction against Expressionism. In 1927, Dix said, "For me the object comes first, and it is the object that orients [directs] form." He was also involved in the **Dada** movement, which developed in Europe as a reaction to the destruction of World War I and encouraged the use of chance in the making of art. As a professor at the Dresden Academy of Art, Dix did not hide his political beliefs so, like Beckmann, he lost his job when the Nazis came to power and he was labeled a **degenerate.** Dix continued to fight the Nazis. In 1939, he was sent to prison for plotting to kill Hitler.

Beckmann continued to paint in the hospital for the next two years, trying to make sense of the horrors he had seen. He moved from painting biblical scenes to painting scenes of human cruelty and torture. He crowded many figures and objects into his paintings. These twist and come out at the viewer, giving a strange, claustrophobic feeling. At a time when other Expressionists were exploring **abstraction,** he decided to be a **history painter.** But he did not record official history for the ruling powers. Instead, he wanted to show the unofficial history— the everyday suffering in European cities.

■ *Carnival*, by Max Beckmann (1920) *Beckmann's work changed after his experiences during World War I. He started to produce harsh, disjointed paintings that differed from his biblical scenes.*

He made large pictures and often used the shapes of religious altarpieces—for example, the three panels of a **triptych**—so that his works were noticed and taken seriously. He became one of Germany's foremost painters, as part of the movement called the **New Objectivity.**

In 1925, at the age of 41, Beckmann was appointed to teach at an art college in Frankfurt. That same year he divorced Minna and married Mathilde von Kaulbach, whom he featured in many of his important paintings. In 1929, he was promoted to professor. Over the next four years, he had several major exhibitions and awards for his artistic achievements. In 1933, the Nazis came to power and, because Beckmann's art was so political, they fired him from his professorship. Along with that of the other Expressionists, the Nazis considered his work to be socially and morally corrupt and labeled him a **degenerate.** He moved then to Berlin to attract less attention. In 1937, the Nazis confiscated 590 of his paintings from German museums. He became afraid for his safety and fled to Holland with his wife. Perhaps to express his anger, he wrote an article called "My Theory of Painting," which was more about the politics of the time than about painting. Holland was not an easy place to live either, as it suffered **German occupation** and poverty during World War II. After the war was over, Beckmann was able to emigrate to the United States, where he taught in Washington and New York. By this time, he was widely accepted as one of the major forces in twentieth-century art. He continued to paint until his death in New York City, in 1950.

George Grosz (1893–1959)

Grosz was another member of the New Objectivity movement. Although he believed in a new **objectivity,** he was also interested in an art that did not make sense. He helped set up the Club **Dada** in Berlin, editing its magazine and organizing a Dada fair. Like Dix, Grosz was very critical of the idea of military power, and although he had fought in World War I, he was not an enthusiastic volunteer. He had been dismissed as unfit for service and was put on trial for attacking an officer. To show his disgust for his German nationality, he and a friend, John Heartfield (originally Helmut Herzfeld), changed their names to English spellings. They sent each other postcards with small collages that hid criticisms of Germany. In 1931, he moved to New York to be a teacher. He stayed there to escape the Nazis, who labeled him a degenerate. In 1959, he returned to West Berlin, saying, "My American dream turned out to be a soap bubble." In other words, Grosz felt that he had failed to make much of a name for himself in the United States. He died in Berlin in 1959 as the result of a bad fall.

James Ensor (1860–1949)

- Born April 13, 1860 in Ostend, Belgium
- Died in 1949 in Ostend, Belgium

Key works
Woman Eating Oysters, 1882
The Entry of Christ into Brussels, 1888
Skeletons Warming Themselves, 1889

James Ensor made some paintings before 1900 that showed signs of Expressionism. This was before the Expressionist movement began. His work made a big impression on Paul Klee, who owned an etching by him.

Ensor's father was English and his mother was Belgian. He had a younger sister, Mariette. Their parents owned a souvenir shop, where the talented and imaginative boy grew up among grotesque masks, puppets, and exotic and colorful bric-a-brac. The false faces of these masks and puppets appear in many of his paintings. However, Ensor's imagination was really fired by two of the most famous Belgian artists of all time, Hieronymus Bosch (c.1450–1516) and Pieter Bruegel the Elder (1525–1569). He would have seen copies of their gruesome and comic depictions of monsters and people oddly transformed.

Ensor spent three years studying at the Brussels Academy, from 1877 to 1880. His earliest mature paintings were largely of interior scenes and landscapes in somber colors. This style was a strong contrast to the light, bright work of the Impressionists who were so fashionable at the time. The years 1880–1900 were his most productive, and by age 22, Ensor had exhibited in the Brussels **Salon** and the prestigious Paris Salon.

Ensor was disgusted by the vanity and vulgarity that he witnessed in Ostend's crowds of tourists and began to use them for his subject matter. The following year his painting called *Woman Eating Oysters* was refused by the salons. It was the first of many works that would be considered too controversial for public taste. He had by now begun to reintroduce the masks and skeletons of his early work and used them to criticize the behavior of the society in which he lived. His *Cathedral* shows a masked crowd acting out a **parody** of a religious festival. It is a criticism of the people's insincerity rather than of the Catholic Church.

In 1883, the **Twenty Group** was formed, and Ensor exhibited at their first salon in 1884. His influence on the group waned with the increasing popularity of French art. He was expelled from the group in 1889 after the public outrage at his painting *The Entry of Christ into Brussels*.

Ensor was an isolated, often unhappy figure but an extremely original artist. He continued to paint subjects that criticized his country, the Church, and the king. Nevertheless, in 1929, the king of Belgium made him a baron, an important honor. Ensor had by then been accepted as an artist of international importance and is today regarded as one of the founders of Expressionism. He enjoyed his last 20 years in Ostend surrounded by young, admiring writers and artists. He died in 1949.

Self-Portrait with Masks, by James Ensor (1899)
Ensor's early influences were reflected in his paintings of mysterious, sometimes frightening masks and pictures overcrowded with people.

Wassily Kandinsky (1866–1944)

- Born December 4, 1866 in Moscow, Russia
- Died December 13, 1944 at Neuilly-sur-Seine, France

Key works

Cossacks, 1910-1911
Improvisation on No. 19, 1911
With a Black Arc, 1912
Dreamy Improvisation, 1913

Kandinsky was 30 years old before he began to study art, but he still had a long and successful career as an artist. He is important because he made some of the first experiments in **abstraction.**

Wassily Kandinsky was born in 1866 into a wealthy Russian family. His father ran a tea company in Moscow. He went to nursery school in Florence, Italy, but when his father's health worsened in 1871, the family moved back to Odessa, Russia. Shortly afterward, Kandinsky's parents divorced and he was brought up by his aunt.

Kandinsky had a busy childhood. His parents were musical, and Kandinsky took piano and cello lessons from an early age. His love of color and shape was influenced by watercolors that his aunt gave him. He took art lessons, too, and was encouraged to draw and paint in his spare time by both his aunt and his father. He continued to take extra lessons in art and music in high school but he did not think of either subject as a possible career.

He began his adult life studying economics and law from 1886 to 1892 at Moscow University. In his final year of school, Kandinsky married his cousin, Ania Tchimiakin, and worked as a teacher of law at Moscow University. Later, he managed an art-printing factory and was offered a teaching position at the University of Tartu in Estonia, which he refused. Compared to art, his career seemed dull and heavy. He finally made his decision to give up his career when he saw an exhibition featuring the Impressionist artist, Monet. Kandinsky was excited by a painting of a haystack. It showed him that art was not dependent on an interesting subject. Instead, an artist could shock and impress a viewer by using new ways of applying paint. Kandinsky had not even realized that the picture was of a haystack until he read the catalog.

This photograph of Wassily Kandinsky was taken in Munich, Germany in 1913.

In 1896 Kandinsky moved to Munich, a center of artistic activity, to study art with the realist artist Anton Azbe. However, Kandinsky was mature and ambitious—he wanted to learn as much as he could as quickly as possible. He was frustrated by Azbe's emphasis on painting models. So, he spent a year working from home and in the outdoors, exploring color. He wanted to be at the Munich Academy of Art, a popular and important art school, in the drawing class taught by renowned teacher Franz von Stuck. After two attempts, Kandinsky was accepted to the Munich Academy in 1900. Although he felt he learned much from von Stuck himself, he found the whole atmosphere of the Academy frustrating, saying it was "the most certain means to kill off childhood genius."

In 1901, Kandinsky left the Academy and co-founded the Phalanx group of artists, who ran an art school and put on exhibitions until 1904. One of these

■ *Cossacks*, by Wassily Kandinsky (1910-1911)
Kandinsky's Expressionist phase included paintings, such as Cossacks, *which illustrated his love of primary colors. He thought that pure colors could powerfully influence people to the extent that the subject of the painting was of little importance.*

exhibitions, in 1903, showed sixteen canvases by Monet. Kandinsky was making woodcut prints and designing clothing and posters in the *Jugendstil,* or "young style" fashion that was then popular in Germany. His paintings at this time were landscapes based on folk tales. He was very successful, winning prizes and exhibiting all over Europe.

Kandinsky's marriage to Ania failed in 1903. In 1902, he had met the woman who was to be his second partner, the painter Gabriele Münter. Over the next six years he traveled, often with her, to Italy, Holland, France, Switzerland, Tunisia, and Russia. He returned to live in Munich in 1908. In the summer, he and Gabriele visited Murnau, a small town in the country in southern Germany, which they found restful and inspiring. The next year, Gabriele bought a house there. It became her permanent home and Kandinsky visited regularly. Their friends Marianne von Werefkin and Alexei von Jawlensky, also artists, lived and painted there with them. Kandinsky's colors become more primary and his shapes stronger. One day, he saw one of his paintings lying on its side but still looking strong and beautiful. This encouraged him to work on color and shape without clear subjects. He was moving toward **abstraction,** which he achieved by 1913.

In 1910, Kandinsky made friends with Franz Marc, one of the few people to express admiration for Kandinsky's new work. A year later, they formed a magazine called *Der Blaue Reiter.* Kandinsky published his first book, *Concerning the Spiritual in Art,* in 1912. The book was about his theories that shape and color could express **spiritual** meanings. It was a success at the time, and is still read by students studying art.

Kandinsky was forced to return to Russia in 1914 because of World War I. Germany was fighting against Russia in the war, so as a Russian citizen, he could not stay in Germany. In 1916, he separated from Münter. Kandinsky was well-connected in Russia because of his family, so after the Revolution in 1917, he worked in a series of high-level government jobs to develop culture. He co-founded the Moscow Academy of Arts. However, he disagreed with the main idea in Russia that industrial design was more important than fine art, so he went back to Germany.

Kandinsky taught at the Bauhaus in Weimar and Dresden from 1922 to 1933. By then, Kandinsky was painting in a purely abstract manner. In 1933, when the Nazis came to power and the Bauhaus was shut down, he left Germany to live in Neuilly-sur-Seine, near Paris, where he died in 1944.

Ernst Ludwig Kirchner 1880–1938

- Born May 6, 1880 in Aschaffenburg, Germany
- Died June 15, 1938 in Davos, Switzerland

Key works

Street, Berlin, 1913
Five Women in the Street, 1913
The Drinker (Self-Portrait), 1915
Self-Portrait as a Soldier, 1915

The Drinker (Self-Portrait), by Ernst Kirchner (1915)
Kirchner suffered a mental and physical breakdown as a result of World War I. He later said he painted The Drinker *in Berlin "while screaming military convoys were passing beneath my window day and night."*

Kirchner was the brains behind the artists' group *Die Brücke*. He was a handsome man and a natural leader, but he was also moody and vain. This caused some lost friendships. He was a workaholic, producing thousands of paintings, prints, and designs in his lifetime.

Ernst Ludwig Kirchner was born in 1880 in Germany to Maria Elise and Ernst Kirchner. He had two younger brothers, Hans Walter and Ulrich. Kirchner went to grade school in Chemnitz, where two of his fellow pupils were Erich Heckel and Karl Schmidt-Rottluff. Kirchner showed an early talent in art, which his parents praised and encouraged from the start. However, they opposed his wish to make art his career. Following his father's wishes, he studied architecture at the Technical School in Dresden from 1901 to 1903. The year 1903–1904 was a significant time for Kirchner, when he attended an experimental art school in Munich and saw many exhibitions of French art. While in Munich he made a trip to nearby Nuremberg. He saw the work of the fifteenth-century artist Albrecht Dürer—one of the greatest printmakers in art history. Kirchner was so inspired by Dürer's prints that he decided he wanted to become an artist. However, he needed to earn his degree, so he returned to the Technical School in Dresden and graduated in architecture in 1905. It was there that he made friends with Fritz Bleyl, and later rediscovered Erich Heckel and Karl Schmidt-Rottluff. The four became close when they discovered they all had more of an interest in fine art than architecture.

Erich Heckel (1883–1970) and Karl Schmidt-Rottluff (1884–1976)

Heckel and Schmidt-Rottluff were two important founding members of *Die Brücke*. They went to the same school as Kirchner in Chemnitz, but because they were four years younger than Kirchner they did not know him. It was not until Heckel went to Dresden in 1904 to study architecture that he became friends with Kirchner. Later Schmidt-Rottluff came to Dresden, also to study architecture, but he left the school after only one year.

Heckel was enthusiastic and self-confident. His energy kept the group together. It was also in Heckel's studio, in an old butcher's shop, that the group worked. However, it was Schmidt-Rottluff who invented the name *Die Brücke*. Schmidt-Rottluff was less enthusiastic than Kirchner and Heckel about working communally in the same studios or on their trips to the lakes. Many of his paintings from the time are landscapes with no figures, some painted on the North Sea coast or in Norway. You can see the connection with Emil Nolde, whom Schmidt-Rottluff introduced to the group. In 1914, he turned to painting figures, often sad-looking women, to express the gloom of life in Germany at the time. He also began making wooden figures inspired by African sculptures. He served in the war from 1915 to 1918.

On June 7, 1905, Kirchner and his three friends founded *Die Brücke*. Kirchner wrote their **manifesto.** In 1908, they exhibited with the ***Fauves,*** and Kirchner's paintings became brighter and bolder. The exhibition was well-received by the public, but Kirchner's parents were dismayed at their son's choice of career. They continued to disapprove in the years to come, although they helped out on the occasions when Kirchner was forced to ask them for money.

A Group of Artists, by Ernst Kirchner (1926)
Painted some time after the breakup of Die Brücke, *Kirchner wanted to portray the friendship that had at first existed between the artists. It is noticeable however that Heckel is painted between the figures of Kirchner and Schmidt-Rottluff, the two most opposite members of* Die Brücke.

It was mainly Kirchner's idea that the group spend summers out of Dresden to paint and live closer to nature. People's relationship to the natural world was an important influence to the members of *Die Brücke*. In 1908, Kirchner visited the Isle of Fehmarn in the Baltic Sea with his girlfriend, Emmy Frisch, and her brother. The bleakness of the sea made a strong impact on him. In the summers of 1909, 1910, and 1911 he and the group often went to the Moritzburg lakes to paint, taking other friends and models. Kirchner's romantic view of nature was replaced by an excitement for the city when, in 1911, he moved from Dresden to Berlin. He wanted to show the tough and uncompromising nature of the city life he was surrounded by, so his style became less decorative and exotic and more gritty and realistic. For example, he now painted prostitutes and street scenes in which people merge with buildings. This perhaps reflects his state of mind in that he felt alone and unstable in Berlin, less close to his *Die Brücke* friends. He met Erna Schilling, who was to become his lifelong partner.

Kirchner published a history of *Die Brücke* in 1913 and this caused its breakup. As he told the story, he had generated all the new ideas and the others had copied him. The others said he had been too dominating. Later, he tried to say that the *Die Brücke* phase of his life had not been important to his development. When World War I began, he signed up for military service but described himself as an "involuntary volunteer." The service did not suit him. Only a year later, he was discharged, unable to cope with army life. In 1916, he wrote about the horrors that he had experienced during the war: "The heaviest burden of all is the pressure of war and the increasing superficiality [shallowness]. It gives me incessantly the impression of a bloody carnival. I feel as though . . . everything is topsy-turvy." He suffered a mental breakdown and spent three years recovering in hospitals. He believed that if he got well, he would be made to fight again, so he resisted the healing process, growing dependent on sleeping pills, morphine, and alcohol. He did, however, continue to paint and make woodcuts of the hospitals he was kept in.

Kirchner's friends encouraged him to live in a healthier place than the city. So, in 1918, accompanied by a nurse, he rented a farm near Davos in Switzerland. His partner, Erna, remained in Berlin to look after his studio. In Davos, surrounded by local farmers, he rediscovered the community spirit he had been searching for and he returned to natural themes in his paintings. He described his love for the landscape there in 1919: "There was such a wonderful setting of the moon this morning, the yellow moon against little pink clouds, and the mountains a pure, deep blue." A few years later, he moved to Wildboden in Switzerland and continued to paint. He had some major exhibitions in Switzerland. However, his success and the peace of his living situation were no defense against the Nazis. In 1937, they labeled him a **degenerate** and confiscated 639 of his works from museums in Germany, selling some abroad and destroying others. He tried to make his position safer by applying for Swiss citizenship for himself and Erna. But he became more and more depressed while waiting for a response, and he committed suicide in 1938.

Paul Klee (1879–1940)

- Born December 18, 1879 at Munchenbuchsee, Switzerland
- Died June 29, 1940 at Muralto-Locarno, Switzerland

Key works
In the Houses of St. Germain (Tunis), 1914
Zoo, 1918
Senecio, 1922
Carnival in the Mountains, 1924

Paul Klee is a unique and major artist who produced about 8,000 works of art. His work is so imaginative and delicate it is unlike the other Expressionists. However, he was happy to work under the banner of Expressionism because he wanted to find ways to "make visible what has been perceived in secret." This means he wanted to express the feelings created in him by the world he saw around him rather than make an exact copy of them.

Paul Klee was born on December 18, 1879 in Switzerland. His mother, Ida Maria, was Swiss and his father, Hans, was German. They were both musicians, although his father worked as a teacher. Paul inherited his father's sense of humor. He also became a talented violinist. He had a sister, Mathilde. Klee also had another special talent—he was ambidextrous. He drew with his left hand and wrote with his right. As a schoolboy, Klee was popular because of his wit. He drew constantly, even throughout lessons. Common subjects for his drawings were plants, cats, birds, and fish. He did well only in music, poetry, and art at school, so it was obvious that he was going to be an artist of some sort. Like Kandinsky, who came from Russia to study in Munich, Klee wanted to leave his homeland of Switzerland to study in the city where experimental artists were gathering. At the age of nineteen, he started at Knirr's Art School. It was around this time that he first met his future wife, pianist Lily Stumpf. In 1900, the same year as Kandinsky, Klee was accepted by the Munich Academy of Fine Art, and took Franz von Stuck's class. He struggled with color. He did not receive much help from von Stuck, who even suggested he should stop painting and become a sculptor instead. However, he did learn a great deal in 1901 by traveling around Italy to see art with his friend, sculptor Hermann Haller. In Italy, Klee was especially amazed by the work of Leonardo da Vinci.

Because Klee was not earning money as an artist, he went home to Berne in 1902, where he could play the violin in an orchestra while he developed his art. A trip to Paris in 1905 opened his eyes to modern French art, but he said he had nothing to learn from it. Although his technique was steadily improving, he was still struggling to express himself in his paintings in the way that he wished. Some pictures he did exhibit at this time were criticized for their "mad anatomy"—the forms were considered grotesque and misshapen. In 1906 he married Lily and they settled in a small apartment in Munich. Lily gave piano lessons while Paul continued with his art. In 1907, they had a son, Felix. Paul, still an unknown artist, acted as househusband while Lily earned money with her teaching.

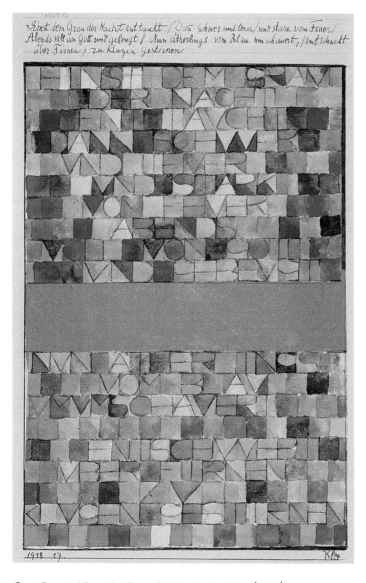

▮▮▮ *Once Emerged from the Gray of Night*, by Paul Klee (1918)
Klee often used letters and numbers in his work to try to link dreams and reality.

In 1908, Klee saw two van Gogh exhibitions and was stunned by the expression of Van Gogh's emotion in his paintings. However, Klee did not feel he had that level of tragic passion in himself to put into his work. Klee was affected in the same way by James Ensor, whose work he received from a friend in Berne. A year later, in 1909, he saw a Cézanne exhibition for the first time and said, "He is my teacher par excellence, much more so than van Gogh," perhaps because Cézanne's paintings are so carefully constructed and are less a show of emotion.

In 1909, Klee's pictures came more from his imagination and dreams, in a process that he called "psychic improvisation." He still liked to draw and paint from nature, but more and more he wished to express the feelings that natural objects inspired in him, rather than represent the objects themselves.

In 1910, Klee had some success with an exhibition that toured Switzerland and Munich. In 1911, he met August Macke, who introduced him to Kandinsky. Klee also made friends with Franz Marc. He took part in the second exhibition of *Der Blaue Reiter*. These artists were all interested in the use of color and greatly influenced Klee. He began to study pure color—not as it appears in nature but as unmixed paint colors placed next to each other to create effects. The artists he was now working with introduced him to the work of the artist Robert Delaunay, whom he met in Paris in 1912. Klee was strongly influenced by Delaunay and translated his writings about windows and light for publication in Germany.

In 1914, Klee made a happy visit to Tunis in North Africa with Macke. He said then, "Color has got me . . . color and I are one. I am a painter." He meant that he finally understood the meaning of color and that he could at last be a proper painter. He stored many images in his memory and they came out in his art over many years. He served in World War I, but he did not fight on the front. He spent much of the time painting airplane wings and found plenty of time for his own work. However, he was very upset by the death of his closest friend, Marc, during the war.

Robert Delaunay (1885–1941)

Robert Delaunay was a French painter who developed the movement called Orphism, a branch of Cubism that gave priority to the use of rich, exciting color. Equally important in its development was his wife, painter and textile designer Sonia Delaunay-Terk. They explored the links between color and movement, and their work became very **abstract** by 1912. Marc and Macke had seen Delaunay's window pictures and liked the way the scenes were broken up as if seen through a prism. Together with Klee and some other Expressionists, they adopted certain aspects of Delaunay's work, introducing fragmented geometric shapes and split planes into their paintings, which made them appear more abstract.

A major 1919 exhibition in Munich showed 362 of Klee's paintings, and made him internationally famous. In 1920, the founder of the Bauhaus school of design, Walter Gropius, invited him to teach there. He moved with his family, following the various homes of the Bauhaus until 1930, when he left to teach at the Düsseldorf Art Academy. While at the Bauhaus, Klee became very inspirational as a teacher and a writer of theories on art. When the Nazis rose to power and declared all Expressionist art **degenerate,** Klee campaigned against this idea, which led to his dismissal from the Düsseldorf Academy in 1933. He returned to Berne, depressed by the political situation, and his art became darker in both color and content. He began to suffer from scleroderma, a rare disease that causes hardening of certain areas of the body, such as the skin, heart, and lungs. He died from the disease in 1940. He continued to paint until the very end.

III *Paul Klee is shown here in 1921, not long after he began teaching at the Bauhaus in Berlin.*

Oskar Kokoschka (1886–1980)

- Born March 1, 1886 at Pöchlarn, Austria
- Died February 22, 1980 in Villeneuve, Switzerland

Key works

Murderer, Hope of Women, 1909
Portrait of Herwarth Walden, 1910
The Temptation of Christ, 1911-1912
The Tempest or *The Bride of the Wind*, 1914
The Emigrés, 1916-1917

More than any other artist in this book, Kokoschka stuck to Expressionism throughout his long life. He was a sensitive person who came to painting, despite his training in decorative arts, as a way to communicate his feelings. He suffered from neuralgia, a disease that causes pain in nerves, and transferred his constant pain into figures in his paintings by making their nerves visible as scratchy lines. However, his life decisions were driven as much by the need to earn a living as by his emotion.

Oskar Kokoschka was born in 1886 at Pöchlarn, Austria. His father, Gustav, was a goldsmith from an upper-class family in Prague, Czechoslovakia. His mother, Romana, was the daughter of an imperial forester in Styria. It was from her that Oskar inherited his love of nature. Oskar was the second son of four children, but his older brother had died at an early age. He wanted to be a research chemist to comply with his father's wishes, but a teacher at the School of **Applied Art** in Vienna had been impressed by his drawings and recommended him for a scholarship. He started there in 1905, at age nineteen. He intended to be an art teacher. Kokoschka wrote that the curriculum there was about skill in drawing "leaves and flowers and stems, twisting about like dragons. Drawing the human figure was taboo." He also learned calligraphy, printmaking, and bookbinding, but not painting.

In 1906, Kokoschka saw a van Gogh exhibition and decided he preferred the intensity of portraits to decorative patterns. He set up opportunities to paint the human figure by employing models. He chose thin models, especially circus children, so he could see all their joints and muscles. He continued his craft activities because he needed to earn money. From 1907 to 1909, he was a member of the **Weiner Werkstätte,** where he could design tapestries, illustrate books and, most helpful, exhibit them. He wrote a play called *Murderer, Hope of Women*, which caused a scandal at its first performance in 1909 because of its violence and unstructured style. His poster for the play was so expressive that it was noticed by an architect, Adolf Loos. Loos said he would provide money and commissions if Kokoschka would leave the Weiner Werkstätte. Loos introduced Kokoschka to many Viennese intellectuals and artists, and Kokoschka began to paint their portraits. Unfortunately, some sitters refused to buy their portraits as they were not very flattering or realistic. They called Kokoschka a "soul-ripper" because he did not always paint people as they thought they should look, but seemed to expose the soul.

In 1910, Kokoschka moved to Berlin, which had become an important artistic center. Loos had found him work on a magazine called *Der Sturm* (The Storm). He painted more portraits. He also became known for his work on *Der Sturm*, with its editor, Herwarth Walden. Kokoschka said, "I founded the first German magazine for contemporary art. I was its graphic artist, poet, theatre critic, advertising manager, and distributor." However, despite making a name for himself, he was making very little money.

The Power of Music, by Oskar Kokoschka (1918)
Kokoschka taught art at the Dresden Academy from 1919 to 1924. During this time, he painted The Power of Music.

Only a year later, tired of his life of poverty and hardship, he returned home to Vienna to earn a steady income as an assistant professor at the School of **Applied Art.** He continued to exhibit in Germany and contribute to *Der Sturm*. People in Vienna were not ready for his difficult art. An exhibition there, which included his work, was badly received by art critics in 1911.

Kokoschka fell in love with Alma Mahler, the widow of the famous composer Gustav Mahler. This was the first time he had been deeply involved with a woman. He traveled to Italy with her in 1913, where he was inspired by the Venetian artists Titian and Tintoretto. This romantic time ended in 1914, when he volunteered to fight in World War I. He was seriously wounded a year later. He spent a long time in a military hospital recovering from a head wound and lung injury, but he was not affected mentally by the war. In 1917, he moved to Dresden, where he continued to paint. But he struggled with his injuries, particularly the damage to his ear caused by a bullet passing through his head. It affected his balance for many years. He was also lonely, so he spent his time making a life-sized doll. He considered this work of art a friend and a model, painting it over and over again. He was finally achieving success with his art, and was given a professorship at the Dresden Academy of Art in 1919. Although in later years his paintings sold for large sums of money, he never became very wealthy. He continued to give much of what he earned to his family.

When he found out that he was going to be made the director of the Academy of Art, he was unhappy. He did not want to take on so much administrative responsibility, so he suddenly decided to leave Dresden and his professorship. From 1923 until his death in 1980, Kokoschka lived in five different countries.

He went to Switzerland and then returned home to Vienna when he heard his father was seriously ill. After his father died, Kokoschka moved to Paris. He made daily visits to the Louvre, one of the world's most famous art museums, to see the work of other artists, but did little work himself. He then went on many painting trips around Europe, North Africa, and the Middle East, until 1933 when he returned to Vienna. A year later, he moved to Prague in Czechoslovakia, where his sister was living. Here he met Olda Pavlovska, who later became his wife. In 1938, he had to escape the Nazis, who had branded him a **degenerate.** He and Olda emigrated to London as refugees. In 1947 he became a British citizen. In 1953, he moved to his final home in Villeneuve, near Lake Geneva, Switzerland. Despite failing eyesight, he continued to paint and draw until he died in 1980, a week before his 94th birthday.

■ *This photograph of Oskar Kokoschka was taken in his studio in Villeneuve.*

Käthe Kollwitz (1867–1945)

- Born July 8, 1867 in Königsberg, East Prussia (now Russia)
- Died April 22, 1945 at Moritzburg Castle, near Dresden, Germany

Key works

A Weavers' Uprising, series, 1893–1897
The Peasants' War, series, 1902–1908
Widows and Orphans, 1919
War Memorial at Diksmuide, Flanders, 1932—called "The Parents' Monument"
Death, series, 1934-1935

Käthe Kollwitz had a strong desire to work as an artist, at a time when women were expected only to make art as a hobby. She became a well-known artist, partly because of her professionalism and political activity, and partly because her art is deeply moving.

Kollwitz was born in Königsberg in 1867, the third of four children. She had an older brother, Konrad, and an older sister, Julie. She also had a younger sister, Lise, to whom she was very close. Her parents, Karl and Katherine Schmidt, had strong moral and social beliefs. Her father was a stone mason. Kollwitz said, "From my childhood on, my father had expressly wished me to be trained for a career as an artist, and he was sure there would be no great obstacles to my becoming one." She studied with the engraver Rudolf Mauer from the age of fourteen.

At the age of seventeen, Kollwitz enrolled at the School for Women Artists in Berlin, since women could rarely enter the main art schools. She was influenced at this time by the work of Max Klinger, particularly his series *A Life,* and by the writings of Emile Zola. It was at this point that she first began to use etchings and lithography to depict social injustices.

In 1891, she married Karl Kollwitz, a doctor who worked in one of the slum districts of Berlin. They were both passionately concerned about poverty in the slums around them and the injustice of the spread of wealth in Berlin. Kollwitz tried to challenge society's acceptance of this inequality through her art. There were two ways in which she tried to reach a wide public with this message. One was to make prints or posters that could be multiplied and sold cheaply.
The other was always to make images of people whose poses and faces expressed strong emotion. She used a simple, powerful, and bold style to get her message across as clearly as possible. The pictures that brought her success in 1899 were a series of six prints, *A Weavers' Uprising*. These were inspired by a play by Hauptmann.

In 1898, she became the first woman to teach at the School for Women Artists. This was a measure of her success, given that few other women taught in art schools. In 1904, she studied sculpture at the Académie Julien, in Paris, France, where she met sculptor Rodin. She won the Villa Romana prize in 1907, which allowed her to travel to Florence, Italy. In 1909, she returned to Germany and contributed illustrations to an art journal called *Simplizissimus*. She became increasingly involved in socialist politics. In 1910, she concentrated on making sculptures for a time.

Just after the start of World War I, Kollwitz's youngest son, Peter, was killed in action. This was a personal tragedy, but she did not wallow in her grief. It made her even more determined to show how working people were exploited to fight their governments' wars and expand their industries.

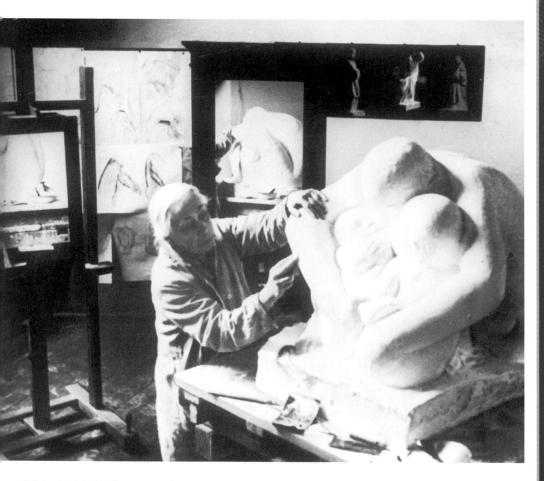

■ *In 1932, Kollwitz was photographed working on the sculpture* Mother with Her Two Children. *One of the main themes of her work was the mother and child.*

Kollwitz wanted to depict the human suffering and emotion caused by war. She showed the effects of war and loss particularly on women and children—for example, in her works *Widows and Orphans* (1919) and *The Survivors* (1923). Other artists, such as Beckmann, Grosz, and Dix, were moved to express antiwar feelings in their work, to present a stark, honest, sometimes shocking view of their times. However, more than any other artist of her time, Kollwitz was anxious to show the terrible suffering of the postwar years.

Kollwitz was often asked to produce posters for aid organizations in order to increase awareness of the problems Germany was suffering at the time. In 1920, Kollwitz joined the famous scientist Albert Einstein, George Grosz, and others to form International Workers Aid (IAH), for which she produced posters such as *Help Russia* and *Vienna is Dying! Save her Children!* She said, "I would like to exert influences in these times when human beings are so perplexed and in need of help," meaning she wanted to guide people to her way of thinking.

In 1926, Kollwitz and her husband visited their son's grave in Belgium. Kollwitz finally completed the memorial figure for Peter in 1931, and it was displayed in the spring exhibition at the Academy in Berlin before being moved to Belgium. The memorial drew much admiration and established Kollwitz as a sculptor as well as a graphic artist.

In the 1920s and early 1930s, Kollwitz was a respected and active member of the art world. She was director of master classes for graphic arts, and by 1928 she became the first woman department head at the Prussian Academy of Arts in Berlin. This came to an end when the Nazis rose to power. She had to resign from the Academy because in 1932 she had signed an appeal of unity against the Nazis, bringing to their attention her anti-Nazi feelings. However, because her art was small scale and could be printed in journals, she could continue to make statements about war and power—for example, with her series of eight prints, *Death* (1934-1935).

Her work was not officially labeled **degenerate,** but she was banned from exhibiting. Unlike other artists of the time, Kollwitz remained in Berlin during the war despite living and working in the middle of the Allied bombing zone. When World War II came, history repeated itself when her grandson, named Peter after her son, was killed. Her husband Karl died in 1940. In 1943, her home and studio were bombed and much of her life's work was destroyed. She lived in virtual seclusion from 1933 until her death, at Moritzburg Castle near Dresden, just a few weeks before the war ended in 1945.

■ *Woman Remembering II*, by Käthe Kollwitz (1920)
*Kollwitz produced many self-portraits throughout her life. This one was
made around the time she became the first woman to be elected to the
Berlin Academy of Art.*

August Macke (1887–1914)

- Born January 3, 1887 in Meschede, Germany
- Died September 26, 1914 in Champagne, France

Key works
Zoological Garden I, 1912
Large, Well-lit Shop Window, 1912
Lady in a Green Jacket, 1913
Girls Among Trees, 1914

August Macke was an important member of *Der Blaue Reiter*, and his colorful paintings were well-liked. His work is less **abstract** than other *Blaue Reiter* artists, but it might have become more so had he lived longer.

August Macke was born in 1887 in Meschede, Germany. His father, August Friedrich Hermann, was a building engineer and his mother, Florentine, was the daughter of a farmer. He had one older sister, Ottilie. Macke began to draw at the

August Macke, by Maler (1906)
Macke was one of the most prolific Expressionist artists.

age of fifteen and showed early talent. Beginning at the age of seventeen, for two years (1904–1906) he went to the Academy of Art and the School of **Applied Art** in Düsseldorf. He designed sets and costumes for the theater there, using his strong sense of pattern and color. In his second year, he began to make trips abroad to see more art, and in two years he visited Italy, Belgium, Holland, and England. This was rounded off with a trip to Paris in June 1907. He had seen Impressionist art in a book, but wanted to see it for real. He especially liked Manet and Degas. In October 1907, Macke settled again for a year of study at Lovis Corinth's painting school in Berlin, but he could not resist going back to Paris to look at the work of other artists.

In 1909, Macke married Elizabeth Gerhardt, whom he had first met in 1903, when she was fifteen. After a honeymoon in Paris, they lived for a year in the country at Tegernsee, Germany, near Bonn. In this happy time, he painted about 200 pictures. He wrote, "I'm working fearfully hard now. Working, for me, means celebrating everything simultaneously: nature, sunlight, trees, plants, people, animals, flowers and pots, tables, chairs, mountains [and] the reflection of water on growing things."

At the end of that year, he made contact with the New Artists' Association in Munich. He had spotted drawings and prints by Marc in the Brackl Gallery. Excited by them, he searched for Marc and they became friends. In April 1910, Macke's son, Walter, was born, and in November of that year the family returned to Bonn. In 1911, he began to contribute to *Der Blaue Reiter* almanac. In 1912, he travelled with Marc to Paris. There they met Robert Delaunay, an artist whom they both admired and later befriended.

In February 1913, Macke's second son, Wolfgang, was born. Later that year, Macke traveled to Tunisia in North Africa to paint. He had been on a painting trip to Lake Thun in Switzerland and said that he saw the "world as visual poetry." He felt that by seeing a place so different from Europe, it would make this poetic vision even more pure. He went to Tunis in 1914 with Paul Klee, whom he had met in Switzerland. They were there only two weeks, but he created 37 beautiful watercolors in that time. Back home these inspired a series of large paintings. However, he had only six weeks to complete these before he was drafted for military service in World War I. He was killed in action in Champagne on September 26, 1914.

▓ *Kairouan I*, by August Macke (1914)
Macke painted Kairouan I, *along with 37 other paintings, while he was on a two-week trip to Tunisia with Paul Klee. He also made hundreds of drawings during this time.*

Franz Marc (1880–1916)

- Born February 8, 1880 in Munich, Germany
- Died March 4, 1916 in Verdun, France

Key works
Blue Horse, 1911
Red Roe Deer II, 1912
Tiger, 1912
The Fate of the Animals, 1913

Franz Marc is known for his animal paintings and for being a key member of *Der Blaue Reiter*. He believed that artists should look into themselves to make art more **spiritual.**

▌ *Like his friend, August Macke, Marc (photographed in 1912) was killed while fighting in World War I.*

At the time of Marc's birth in 1880, his father, Wilhelm Marc, was a professor of painting at the Munich Academy, although he had trained as a lawyer. His mother, Sophie, was from Alsace in France. He had an older brother, Paul. At first, Marc had wanted to study religion, but he had to put off his studies to do a year of national service. On his return, he decided that he could best develop his spiritual ambitions as a painter. He studied art and philosophy at the Academy of Fine Art in Munich until 1903. In that year, he made his first trips to Paris. The Impressionist paintings he saw there had a profound effect on him. However, he thought art should look inward, rather than depicting outer appearances, as the Impressionists did.

In 1904, Marc decided to leave the Academy. His first animal drawings appeared in 1905. He struggled with his paintings, often destroying them—especially his pictures of people. In 1907, he began studying animal anatomy at the Berlin Zoo, trying to commit it to memory so that he did not have to paint animals from life but could look inward and paint them from his imagination. For three years, he taught anatomy in his studio. In 1906, he married Marie Schnür. But they were unhappy, and the marriage was short-lived. He formed a much happier relationship with Maria Francke a year later, and married her in 1908.

In 1910, Marc had his first exhibition. It was held at the Munich gallery of a dealer named Brackl. The critics liked his work and artists such as Macke made contact with him. They became friends. A relative of Macke's helped Marc, who was struggling financially, by regularly buying paintings from him. In 1911, in collaboration with Kandinsky, von Jawlensky, and Macke, Marc began working on *Der Blaue Reiter*.

An important event for him was a visit with Macke to France in 1912 to meet Robert Delaunay, whose ideas about movement fascinated him. On the other hand, the artist Marc least agreed with was Max Beckmann. They had an ongoing argument in magazine articles, in which Beckmann said that good art was the skilful painting of appearances. But Marc said it was "inner greatness," the expression of the feelings inspired by closely looking at something.

In 1914, Marc volunteered for military service in World War I, believing that war might sweep away the old social and cultural forces and bring in new ones. But he was never to find out if he was right. He was killed on March 4, 1916 at the Battle of Verdun. An exhibition in his memory at the Sturm Gallery in Berlin showed him to be an important artist.

Blue Horse I, by Franz Marc (1911)
Marc was best-known for his animal drawings and painted many pictures of horses at this time. Blue Horse I had an almost magical quality because of the unrealistic colors.

Paula Modersohn-Becker (1876–1907

- Born February 8, 1876 in Dresden, Germany
- Died November 20, 1907 in Worpswede, Germany

Key works
Self-portrait with Amber Necklace, 1906
Nude Girl with Goldfish Bowl, 1906
Still-life with Sunflowers, 1907

Paula Modersohn-Becker sold only three paintings and was hardly known in her lifetime, but her work is seen as very important now. Within her circle, she broke many rules of the time about what art should be. She painted herself nude. She made paintings with a formal strength that set her apart from other artists of her time. Her life is a story of a woman torn between her husband and her desire for independence in her work.

Born on February 8, 1876 in Dresden, Germany, Paula Becker was her parents' third child. She was determined to train as an artist, but her father at first refused to let her. So beginning in 1893, she spent two years training to be a teacher. In 1896, she persuaded her father to support her financially when she was accepted to study drawing and painting at the Society of Women Artists in Berlin.

Self-portrait with Camelia Branch, by Paula Modersohn-Becker (1907)

Probably the most important female artist of her day, Modersohn-Becker produced 750 paintings in her short career.

In 1897, Becker met her future husband, a landscape painter named Otto Modersohn, while living in an artists' colony in Worpswede, near Berlin. The colony was set up in 1884 by Fritz Mackensen. Several artists lived and worked together, learning from Mackensen in an informal way. The colony was set in a bleak but beautiful landscape, and the artists' painting tried to capture this wildness and the simplicity of rural life.

However peaceful she found Worpswede, Becker wanted to learn from other people besides Mackensen, so in January 1900 she went to study in Paris. She had an exciting time and met the artist Emil Nolde. After returning to Worpswede later in the year, she became friends with the poet Rainer Maria Rilke. On May 25, 1901, Becker married Otto Modersohn. The marriage gave her financial security to continue painting, but she was not entirely at one with the other artists in the colony, including her husband. They could not leave behind depth and the rules of perspective as she had. Otto said her style was crude. In his diary of 1903 he wrote, "Paula hates all conventions, and she has now fallen for the mistake of making everything angular, ugly, bizarre and wooden. The colors are great—but the forms! The style! Hands like spoons, noses like [nuts], mouths like gashes, faces like imbeciles. She's attempting too much . . . She won't listen to advice as usual."

These simple forms did not come from a childish lack of skill, however, but from careful research of classical Greek, Egyptian, and Roman art. Becker's subject matter was not invented or fanciful, but included self-portraits and portraits of local rural people, especially women and children.

From 1903 to 1906, she made three long trips to Paris, where, like Kollwitz in 1904, she met the sculptor Rodin and studied at the Académie Julien. This time she was impressed by the **Nabi** artists as well as van Gogh and Cézanne. Her interest in Cézanne suggests that, like him, she cared most about making good, solid paintings and less about making expressive, dramatic scenes.

Moderson-Becker stayed in Paris for a year, from 1906 to 1907, intending to leave her husband for good and devote herself to the challenge of painting. However, Otto joined her in Paris, and they spent the winter there together. In the spring, he persuaded her to return to Worpswede with him because she was pregnant. She was happy to have a baby girl, Mathilde, in November 1907. Sadly, she would not get to know her daughter. She died soon after giving birth.

Edvard Munch (1863–1944)

- Born December 12, 1863 on a farm near Engelhaug, Norway
- Died January 23, 1944 in Oslo, Norway

Key works

Death in the Sick Chamber, 1892
The Scream, 1893
By the Deathbed, 1895
Virginia Creeper, 1898
The Sick Child, 1907

Munch is the most important modern Norwegian painter. He was a major influence on *Die Brücke* artists. He did not call himself an Expressionist, but his pictures express moods very strongly, especially sadness and grief. He wrote: "For as long as I can remember, I have suffered from a deep feeling of anxiety, which I have tried to express in my art."

Soon after Munch's birth in 1863, his family moved to Christiania, now Oslo. His was a distinguished family. On his father's side there were high-ranking churchmen. His Uncle Peter was one of Norway's great historians. His father, Christian, was a military doctor. His mother, Laura, came from a well-to-do farming family. Edvard was the second of five children. Most of what is known about Munch's life comes from his journals and letters written to his sister, Inger, and to his Aunt Karen, who looked after the family after his mother died from tuberculosis in 1868. She was a warm, affectionate substitute mother who encouraged the boy's artistic ability. Her letters to him show her to have been a wise and sympathetic friend through the worst times of his life. Munch's father had been so badly affected by his wife's death that he took to an extreme form of **religious fervor.** Munch wrote of how his father could be playful one moment, then suddenly violent, giving frenzied punishments. He wrote: "In my childhood, I felt that I was always treated unjustly, without a mother, sick, and with threatened punishment in Hell hanging over my head." This shows that he was deeply affected first by the physical illness of his mother and then by the distress of his father, which caused his father to behave so irrationally.

However, there were some brighter moments. Munch enjoyed going with his father to visit patients in the hospital, where he could draw them in bed and learn how to compose small groups of figures.

■ *Munch's life was one of great sadness and grief. These emotions can be traced through many of his paintings.*

Sickness was to become a frequent theme in Munch's work. He had to cope with his own ill health, suffering from asthmatic bronchitis and several severe attacks of rheumatic fever, which badly disrupted his schooling. Then, in 1879, when he was fourteen, his older sister, Sophie, died from the same disease as their mother. Tuberculosis was a slow, painful condition. It must have greatly affected the sensitive boy to watch as another loved one wasted away. Eight years later, Munch began to paint the first of six versions of that scene, called *The Sick Child*. This picture seems quite conventional to us today, but it caused an outrage when it was first exhibited at the Oslo Autumn Exhibition in 1886, because it was totally unlike anything that had came before it.

At seventeen, Munch began to study art formally when his father, having given up hope of him becoming an engineer, allowed him to enter the Oslo State School of Art and Handcraft. The following year, in 1881, he produced his first significant painting, *The Hospital Ward*, which he followed with several portraits and family studies. During the next twenty years, Munch traveled extensively in France, Italy, and Germany. In Paris in 1885 he came under the influence of the Impressionists. From 1890, first the **Nabis,** and then the Post-Impressionists, especially van Gogh and Gauguin, claimed his attention.

All the time, the emotional intensity of Munch's own work anticipated that of the Expressionists. During the 1890s, he began working on a large series of paintings he called *The Frieze of Life* —"a poem of life, love, and death." In 1892, he took 55 pictures to Berlin for an exhibition. They included some of the major *Frieze of Life* paintings and *The Sick Child*. His work caused such an uproar that the exhibition was closed after one week, mainly because of the uncompromising personal subject matter. The art establishment also criticized his technical ability, saying his portraits were "so sloppily daubed that at times it is difficult to identify them as human figures . . . they are an insult to art." The younger artists of Berlin were angry at Munch's treatment and formed themselves into a group called the Berlin **Secession.** Munch remained in Berlin, finding many important friends and gradually gaining general support for his work. In 1902, he exhibited 22 of his *Frieze* paintings, many of which—including *The Kiss* and *The Scream*—he also produced as woodcuts and etchings. These made a great impact, as the emotion could be seen in the wild line that made up the figures as well as in the subject matter.

Munch never married. He always found relationships with women difficult. In 1908, after the painful end of a love affair, combined with overwork and too much alcohol, he suffered a mental breakdown while traveling home to Norway. He spent eight months in a hospital in Copenhagen, Denmark. He wrote, "I would not cast off my illness, for there is much in my art that I owe to it." For a while his colors became brighter. In 1914, back in Norway,

Munch was commissioned to paint a series of large murals for the University Hall of Oslo, depicting the forces of nature, science, and history. He completed these in 1916. Later, as he struggled with illness and self-doubt, his work became anguished, tortured, and full of emotion. After his breakdown, he never left Norway. In 1916, he settled in Ekely, Oslo, and lived a solitary life. His 70th birthday in 1933 was internationally recognized, but his works were considered **degenerate** by the Nazis and removed from German museums. He died peacefully of pneumonia at the age of 80 in 1944, two years after his first exhibition in the United States.

▮▮ *Virginia Creeper*, by Edvard Munch (1898)
Regarded as a pioneer in the Expressionist movement, it is Munch's paintings from the 1890s that the public are most familiar with. Munch's work was exhibited 106 times between 1892 and 1909.

Emil Nolde (1867–1956)

- Born August 7, 1867 in the village of Nolde, in Schleswig, Denmark (now Germany)
- Died April 16, 1956 in Seebüll, Germany

Key works

Child and Big Bird, 1912
Life of Christ, 1911–1912
Devil and Scholar, 1919
In the Lemon Garden, 1920
Dancers, 1920

There were two important influences in Nolde's artistic life. One was living in the flat, lonely landscape near the ocean, which made him feel the power of nature. In his imagination, the cries of birds and animals became colors, and natural forms became strange creatures. The other influence was his strict religious upbringing, which never left him. He said, "When I was a child . . . I made a solemn promise to God that when I grew up I would write a hymn . . . The vow has never been fulfilled. But I have painted a large number of pictures . . . I wonder if they will do instead?"

Born Emile Hansen on August 7, 1867, he took the name of his birthplace, Nolde, in 1901. His parents were farmers, and he had three brothers. Nine generations of his family had eked out a living on the family farm. Not cut out for the farming life of his family, during the late 1880s Emil became an apprentice woodcarver. This took him to Karlsruhe, Germany, where he also attended the local School of Arts and Crafts, then to Berlin, where he drew in the museum and became fascinated by Egyptian art.

In 1892, when he was 25, he went to St. Gallen in Switzerland to teach ornamental drawing. Until then, he knew nothing of contemporary art, but there he discovered Swiss artists Arnold Böcklin and Ferdinand Hodler. He often walked in the mountains to try to capture the feeling he had seen in their work. He painted the highest peaks, imagining faces on them where light and shadow fell. He turned these drawings into a series of postcards, which sold so well that he gave up teaching in 1896 to paint full time.

For the next five years, he traveled—to Dachau, Germany; to Paris, France, where he saw the Impressionists and studied at the Académie Julien; and to Copenhagen, Denmark, where he met and married Ada Vilstrup.

■ *Religion and the natural landscape were major influences on Nolde. He always regretted the fact that none of his paintings were ever on display in a church.*

In 1901, Nolde moved to Berlin with his new wife. Through Ada, who had been an actress in Denmark, he was introduced to the theater. In 1903, they settled on the island of Alsen, where in the summer they lived in a fisherman's hut, and he painted gardens and seascapes in vivid colors. In the winter, they returned to Berlin, where he painted theater scenes. At the age of 38, he exhibited his work at a one-man show in Dresden. Members of *Die Brücke* were excited by Nolde's "tempests of color," and they invited him to join in 1906. Nolde felt that *Die Brücke* had not become the alliance of new artists that he had hoped for, so he chose to leave in 1907. By 1908, he had become a well-known artist.

In 1909, he attempted to form a new group to include the artists Matisse, Beckmann, and Munch, but this failed. He joined the Berlin **Secession** instead. Also in 1909, after suffering a period of severe illness, Nolde began to paint pictures with strong religious themes but often featuring grotesque imagery. These pictures were controversial, however, and the Berlin Secession's rejection of *Pentecost* in 1910 caused Nolde to bitterly attack the Secession and be expelled as a result. So with other *Brücke* artists, including Max Pechstein, he helped to found the New Secession.

In Berlin, Nolde spent a lot of time at the Museum of Anthropology and began to write a book titled *Artistic Expression Among Primitive Tribes*. In 1913, he and Ada were invited to join a scientific expedition to New Guinea, and they journeyed there through Russia, Korea, China, Japan, and the Palau Islands. Like the other Expressionist artists, Nolde was fascinated by African art and other **primitive** art styles with their bold patterns and contrasting colors. He was horrified yet thrilled by the ideas of head-hunting and cannibalism. He sketched constantly throughout the trip. He described how, just in case of trouble, Ada held a gun over him while he painted the people. He also painted large-scale works at this time but many of these were taken by the British at the start of World War I and were not returned to him until many years later.

Nolde spent the early 1920s traveling around Europe. In 1926, Nolde bought a farm in Seebüll, near his birthplace. In 1937, he built a modern house with a large gallery on the farm. However, in the same year, the Nazis removed 1,000 of his pictures from German museums. He was devastated to be branded a **degenerate,** as he considered himself a good German and was a member of the Nazi party. In 1941, the **Gestapo** raided his house and took away everything that enabled him to make art. By 1945, however, he managed to make more than 1,300 small watercolors secretly, and at the risk of imprisonment if discovered. He later named these *Unpainted Pictures*. A further blow to Nolde was the bombing of his Berlin studio, from which only a bundle of charred drawings was saved. He lived at Seebüll until his death at the age of 89. His house is now the Nolde Museum.

■■■ *The Sea III*, by Emil Nolde (1913)

*Nolde's first biographer, Max Sauerlandt, described Nolde's love of the sea:
"Nolde understands the sea like no other painter before him. He sees it not
from the beach or from a boat but as it exists in itself, eternally in motion,
ever changing . . ."*

Max Pechstein (1881–1955)

- Born December 31, 1881 in Eckersbach, Germany
- Died June 29, 1955 in Berlin, Germany

Key works
Horse Fair, 1910
Before the Storm, 1910
Summer in the Dunes, 1911
Palau Islands **Triptych,** 1917

Max Pechstein was the first *Die Brücke* member to become popular—his paintings were not as shocking as those of the other artists. He won the State Prize of Saxony in 1907, and at the time was seen as the leading figure of German Expressionism. However, he is now seen as a minor figure. He differed from the others in that he was the only one with a formal training in the craft of painting. Also, he was from a poorer background and was perhaps more driven to achieve popular success.

The success achieved by Pechstein in his early career was a cause of jealousy for Ernst Kirchner, another member of Die Brücke.

Pechstein's father was a textile worker. Pechstein began taking drawing lessons at the age of fifteen and from 1896 to 1900 was apprenticed to a decorative painter in Zwickau, Germany. Then, for two years he studied at the Dresden School of **Applied Art,** where he won many prizes. He was invited to be a teacher there, but he had ambitions to be a fine artist, so he decided to study at the Academy of Fine Arts in Dresden (1902–1906). In 1906, Pechstein joined *Die Brücke* after meeting Erich Heckel. Pechstein had been angry because workers installing a mural of his had toned down a red tulip field with gray. Heckel had appeared at his side and shouted in his support.

In 1907, Pechstein won a scholarship from the Dresden Academy that allowed him to travel to Italy for the first time. He also went to France to see the Fauvists' work. He then moved to Berlin to be in the heart of the established art world. He became a member of the Berlin **Secession** and exhibited with them in 1909, with some success. In 1910, Pechstein's work and that of 26 other artists was refused by the Secession. He helped to found the New Secession, which included the *Brücke* members and *Blaue Reiter* painters.

A year later, he set up an art school called the MUIM Institute, with Ernst Kirchner. He also got married and spent his honeymoon in Italy. All this time, he was still a member of *Die Brücke*. Most of the members of *Die Brücke* had moved to Berlin by 1912. The other members had made a pact to have nothing to do with the more traditional Berlin Secession. When Pechstein exhibited with the Secession, they asked him to leave *Die Brücke*.

In the Dresden Ethnological Museum, Kirchner had discovered the carvings of the Palau Islanders. Pechstein liked them, too, and wanted to experience such a culture for himself. In 1914 he traveled with his wife to the Palau Islands in Micronesia. His time there ended when World War I began. He was captured by the Japanese, sent back to Germany via the the United States, where his wife remained, and drafted into the army. As with many artists who survived their military service, he had a mental breakdown.

Pichstein recovered from his illness and became a member of the Prussian Academy of Arts. In 1933, he was forbidden to paint or exhibit by the Nazis, and he was later branded a **degenerate.** In 1944, his Berlin apartment was bombed. Many of his paintings were destroyed. After World War II was over, he was able to work and teach freely again. He was a professor in Berlin until his death in 1955.

Red Houses, by Max Pechstein (1923)
Pechstein was considered the most important Expressionist at one time, but he never thought that way about himself. He said, "Art has been and remains the part of my life that brings me happiness."

Egon Schiele 1890–1918

- Born June 12, 1890 in Tulln, Austria
- Died October 31, 1918 in Vienna, Austria

Key works
Grimacing Man (Self-Portrait), 1910
Self-Portrait with Black Clay Vase and Spread Fingers, 1911
Self-Portrait with Head Lowered, 1912
Self-Portrait with Chinese Lantern Plant, 1912

Schiele is now the most well-known Austrian Expressionist, although at first his art was too disturbing to be widely accepted. He was born in Tulln, Austria, where his father, Adolf, was the railroad station master. Of six siblings, only three survived. Schiele always thought himself to be different and at school in Tulln, then in Krems, he spent all his spare time drawing. His mother said that he began to draw at eighteen months.

In 1902, the family moved to Klosterneuberg. Schiele went to the prestigious Abbey School, where he did not succeed in anything except art. He felt the teachers did not understand him. The death of his father, who went insane after a long illness, put more strain on the fourteen-year-old boy. However, things improved when a new art teacher, Ludwig Strauch, encouraged him. He produced some very accomplished drawings. Schiele's new guardian, Uncle Leopold, was annoyed by the boy's poor academic performance, but Strauch persuaded him to let Schiele study at the Vienna Academy of Art.

At that time, artist Gustav Klimt (1862–1918) had a considerable influence on young artists in Vienna. When Schiele met him in 1907, he asked his opinion of a folder of drawings. Klimt was impressed by the work, and the two became lifelong friends. Schiele began to copy Klimt's style, with bold lines and silver and gold paint. He had his first exhibition in Klosterneuberg and then a more important one in Vienna in 1909, the same year that he left the Academy. Two of the works, portraits of his friends Hans Massman and Anton Peschka, the latter of whom married his sister Gerti, clearly show Klimt's influence. Some of the Academy artists who exhibited formed the New Art Group. Schiele was the founder of the group.

Schiele continued to exhibit with and without the New Art Group throughout Austria and Germany. From 1910 on, he developed his own style and his work drew mixed reactions. In 1911, he exhibited with the *Der Blaue Reiter* artists. While recognizing his talent, some people were disturbed by his stretched, skeletal figures and grimacing faces.

Schiele lived an unsettled life, often in poverty. He traveled to his mother's birthplace in Bohemia, then back to Austria, trying to gain the appreciation he felt he deserved. Finally, in 1912 he found a studio and apartment in Vienna. There, in 1914, he met Edith Harms, whom he married in 1915, just days before he was drafted for military service. After training in Bohemia, Schiele returned to Vienna, where he was given guard duties and clerical work. He was allowed to continue painting and exhibiting. The year 1917–1918 was a time of great success. Schiele sold many of the 50 pictures he showed with the Vienna **Secession.** He exhibited in many cities and was praised by critics. Almost all of his work was bought by collectors. His talents were finally recognized.

One sadness for Schiele in February, 1918 was Klimt's death after a stroke. Schiele was with Klimt when he died. In October of that year, an influenza epidemic swept through Europe, killing millions of war-weakened, starving people. It first killed Edith, who was expecting their baby. Three days later Schiele died of the same illness, aged only 28.

▌▌▌ *Self-Portrait with Black Clay Vase and Spread Fingers, by Egon Schiele (1911)*
From 1910–1911, Schiele developed his own style, featuring elongated figures, and his colors became stronger and brighter.

The Next Generation

Expressionism as a movement died off in the early 1920s, although many of the artists continued to be successful. It was partly killed by its own success, because younger artists such as the **Dadaists** saw it as too **conservative,** whereas conservative thinkers and politicians saw it as **decadent.** When Hitler accused the Expressionists of being **degenerate** and stripped German museums of their paintings, many emigrated to America or France, where their art and teaching influenced younger artists.

Kandinsky and Klee were influential as teachers at the Bauhaus in the 1920s and 1930s, and their interest in form rather than content contributed to trends in the art world that lasted until the 1960s. Most Bauhaus students became designers and architects. However, they had a clear awareness of the **aesthetic** values of fine art, which meant that their designs were not only functional but also pleasing to look at.

The Legacy of Expressionism

Expressionism had a big impact in the United States, especially in New York, as European artists emigrated there. Max Beckmann and George Grosz were influential through their teaching in New York in the 1940s. However, Expressionism was not just a European import to the United States, but a

▌▐ *Alchemy*, by Jackson Pollock (1947)
Pollock's style of painting was similar to that of the Expressionist artists because he felt art came from expressing feelings, not representing realistic objects. He said, "Today painters do not have to go to a subject-matter outside themselves."

Jackson Pollock (1912–1956)

Jackson Pollock is well-known for the action painting technique he developed from the mid-1940s. He would lay a canvas on the floor and then drip or pour wet paint onto the canvas from the can. He would make marks with his hands, or sticks or trowels rather than brushes. He seemed to match the stereotype of the Expressionist artist pouring out his strong emotions through his very physical acts of painting.

cross-fertilization between American and various European movements. This was one of the influences on the rich variety of styles covered by the term Abstract Expressionism, which would form in New York City, and come to dominate the art world in the 1950s. Mark Rothko (1903–1970), Barnett Newman (1905–1970), and Clyfford Still (1904–1980) shared Beckmann's interest in large-scale, serious paintings, but like Kandinsky and Klee they wanted color or marks to express emotions and communicate their paintings' meanings to the viewer, rather than realistically represent people and symbolic objects. Rothko, Newman, and Helen Frankenthaler developed a type of painting filled with flat colors, called color-field painting, which can be linked to the **spiritual** importance of color explored by Kandinsky and Klee.

German artists were responsible for bringing about a new tendency toward Expressionism in the 1980s called Neoexpressionism. Since that time, American, British, and Italian artists have become Neoexpressionists as well.

Neoexpressionism in Germany showed the influence of *Die Brücke* and *Der Blaue Reiter* Expressionist styles of the early 1900s. The Neoexpressionists were also influenced by Abstract Expressionists. The best-known German Neoexpressionist is Anselm Kiefer (1945-). He incorporated elements of the art of the German painter Casper David Friedrich, the French sculptor Auguste Rodin, and the Dutch painter Vincent van Gogh.

Anselm Kiefer (1945-)

The German artist Anselm Kiefer is one of the most important artists to appear since the end of World War II. His large-scale paintings reflect the physical and psychological destruction of Germany during World War II. His dark images portray a broken, devastated landscape. Many of his paintings contain photographic images and real objects, such as straw, sand, and copper wires.

Timeline

1860	James Ensor born on April 13
1863	Edvard Munch born on December 12
1866	Wassily Kandinsky born on December 4
1867	Käthe Kollwitz born on July 8
	Emil Nolde born on August 7
1876	Paula Modersohn-Becker born on February 8
1879	Paul Klee born on December 18
1880	Ernst Ludwig Kirchner born on May 6
	Franz Marc born on February 8
1881	Max Pechstein born on December 31
1884	Max Beckmann born on February 12
1886	Oskar Kokoschka born on March 1
1887	August Macke born on January 3
1890	Egon Schiele born on June 12
1903	**Weiner Werkstätte** set up in Vienna

1905	*Fauve* exhibition at the fall **Salon** in Paris
	Die Brücke (The Bridge) group formed by Kirchner, Heckel, Schmidt-Rottluff, and Bleyl
1909	The Berlin **Secession** formed
1911	Kandinsky and Marc form *Der Blaue Reiter*
1913	*Die Brücke* breaks up
1914	World War I begins
1917	Russian Revolution begins
1918	World War I ends
1919	Bauhaus school of art and design opens
1920	First International **Dada** Fair
1928	Kollwitz made first woman department head at the Prussian Academy of Arts in Berlin
1933	Hitler comes to power in Germany
	The Bauhaus closed by the Nazis
1937	The **Degenerate** Art exhibition held
1939–45	World War II

Glossary

abstract   describes a picture with no recognizable subject but which is a composition of shape, color, and line

aesthetic   to do with beauty and the appreciation of beautiful things

applied art   art skills applied to useful activities such as interior design, architecture, furniture design, or commercial graphics. Since the Renaissance it has been considered to be of a lower status than fine art.

avant-garde   art which is forward-looking and experimental

bohemian   describes someone who has rejected the conventional values of society, lives very informally, and dresses in an elaborate and decorative way

conservative   describes someone who conforms to strict social rules, is wary of change and holds cautious, moderate views

cross-fertilization   in art, the interchange of ideas that helps in the spread of a movement or style, for example

Dada   "anti-art" art movement that took place mainly in Zurich and Berlin from 1916. It tried to break down the traditional barriers among art forms. Dada art did not have to make sense. It influenced Surrealism.

decadent   lacking morals; describes someone who just wants to have fun rather than work hard for the establishment society. The German Weimar governments in the 1920s created a climate in which the arts could flourish. However, the Nazis squashed all this from 1933 onward.

degenerate   refers to people and ideas that fall outside the Nazis' narrow vision and was thought to threaten their goal of creating a pure, superior race. They attacked modern art as degenerate, calling it "political and cultural anarchy."

Fauve   Expressionist style of painting inspired by the Post-Impressionists, especially Cézanne, based on intense and vivid colors. It emerged as the first major avant-garde development of the twentieth century. The name, meaning "wild beasts," was coined by a hostile critic in 1905.

German occupation   period of time during World War II when Germany conquered and occupied various European countries

Gestapo   German secret police under the Nazis

history painter   type of artist who told stories in his or her work from the Bible or from classical mythology. History painting had the highest status of all the genres (types of subject matter), compared to still life and landscape painting, because it was intellectual and was intended for display in the most public and grand places. Max Beckmann wanted to create a modern form of this genre.

Jugendstil   German term for Art Nouveau. It was a movement for decorative art and craft and a reaction against history painting.

manifesto   public statement of the policy or aims of a group or society

modernism   international artistic movement that took place around the time of World War I. Modernist artists believed that the traditional order of things had broken down and there was no existing style that could portray the new reality. They therefore looked for new ways to show this in their art.

Nabi from a Hebrew word meaning "prophets," the Nabis were a group of artists formed in 1892 by members of the Académie Julien, Paris, who were influenced by Gauguin. Members included Bonnard, Vuillard, and Denis.

New Objectivity movement in German painting in the 1920s and early 1930s against abstraction and the fragmentation of Cubism. The artists involved, such as Grosz, Dix and Beckmann, thought that art should be more understandable and realistic, less personal and more political, than Expressionism.

objectivity opposite of subjectivity. If you look at things subjectively you color them with your own tastes or feelings. If you are objective, you try to see things without any individual prejudice.

parody exaggerated and humorous imitation of, for example, a work of literature or art, or a style

primitive describes a people or a style that is undeveloped and simple

religious fervor passionate, often extreme and obsessive form of devotion to God

Salon French word for "drawing room." It came to refer to a major annual exhibition in which the members of an art academy showed their latest works. It originated in Paris. When the Impressionists were rejected from the Salons, they opened their independent Salon des Refusés.

secession a splitting off from an organization to form a new group. After 1890, in Munich, Berlin, and Vienna there were a number of secessions formed from the traditional art academies. Younger artists were reacting against art that glorified royalty and establishment society.

spiritual to do with the soul or spirit of a person rather than the body. Can be used to refer to religious or holy things.

triptych painting or relief carving made on three panels, which are hinged together vertically. Used loosely, it can refer to a set of three paintings.

Twenty Group (Les Vingt) society of artists founded in Brussels, Belgium, by Octave Maus. It supported Symbolist and neo-impressionist art in particular. James Ensor was among the first to exhibit with them in 1884.

Weiner Werkstätte (Viennese Workshops) organization of craftspeople and designers set up in Vienna in 1903 to further the ideas and teachings of the great English designer William Morris

Resources

List of Famous Works

Max Beckmann (1884–1950)
Family Scene, 1918, Fine Arts Museum of San Francisco
Self-Portrait with Stiff Hat, etching, 1921, Minneapolis Institute of Arts
Departure, 1932-1933, The Museum of Modern Art, New York

James Ensor (1860–1949)
The Garden of the Rousseau Family, 1885, Cleveland Museum of Art, Ohio
The Entry of Christ into Brussels, 1888, J. Paul Getty Museum, Los Angeles
Skeletons Warming Themselves, 1889, Kimbell Art Museum, Fort Worth, Texas

Wassily Kandinsky (1866–1944)
Blue Mountain, 1908–1909, Guggenheim Museum, New York
Improvisation 30 (Cannons), 1913, Art Institute of Chicago
Angle Rouge, 1928, Musée Maillol, France

Ernst Ludwig Kirchner (1880–1938)
Reclining Nude, 1909, Museum of Fine Arts, Boston
Two Women, 1911, Los Angeles County Museum of Art
Dresden: Schlossplatz, 1926, Minneapolis Institute of Arts

Paul Klee (1879–1940)
Runner at the Goal, 1921, The Guggenheim Museum, New York
The March to the Summit, 1922, San Diego Museum of Art
Red Balloon, 1922, The Guggenheim Museum, New York

Oskar Kokoschka (1886–1980)
Murderer, Hope of Women, 1910, Los Angeles County Museum of Art
Two Nudes, 1913, Museum of Fine Arts, Boston
Portrait of Putnam D. McMillan, 1957, Minneapolis Institute of Arts, Minnesota

Käthe Kollwitz (1867–1945)
Death, Mother and Child 1910, Birmingham Museum of Art, Alabama
Mother and Sleeping Child, 1913, Ball State Museum of Art, Indiana
Woman Remembering II, 1920, Fine Arts Museums of San Francisco

Auguste Macke (1887–1914)
Russian Ballet I, 1912, Kunsthalle Bremen, Germany
Children in a Garden, 1912, Kunstmuseum, Berlin
Seiltänzer, 1914, Kunstmuseum, Berlin

Franz Marc (1880–1916)
Siberian Dogs in the Snow, 1909–1910, National Gallery of Art, Washington
Yellow Cow, 1911, Guggenheim Collection, New York
Colored Flower, 1913-1914, San Diego Museum of Art

Paula Modersohn-Becker (1876–1907)
Portrait of a Woman, 1898, National Gallery of Art, Washington DC
Tree, 1899, Snite Museum of Art at the University of Notre Dame, Indiana
Sitting Old Woman, c.1906, Fine Arts Museums of San Francisco

Edvard Munch (1863–1944)
Starry Night, 1893, J. Paul Getty Museum, Los Angeles
Melancholy (Evening), 1896, Museum of Fine Arts, Boston
Two Women on the Shore, 1898, Art Institute of Chicago

Emil Nolde (1867–1956)
Self-Portrait, 1917, The Detroit Institute of Arts
Still Life, Tulips, 1930, North Carolina Museum of Art
Narcissi and Hyacinths, 1950, San Diego Museum of Art

Max Pechstein (1881–1955)
Early Morning, 1914, Portland Museum of Art, Maine
Exotische Koppe, 1919, California State University Library
After the Bath, c. 1920, The University of Michigan Museum of Art

Egon Schiele (1890–1918)
The Couple, 1915, Carnegie Museum of Art, Pennsylvania
Seated Woman, Back View, 1917, Metropolitan Museum of Art, New York
Portrait of Paris von Gütersloh, 1918, The Minneapolis Institute of Arts

Useful Web Sites

National Gallery of Australia, Canberra
www.nga.gov.au

Solomon R. Guggenheim Museum, New York
www.guggenheim.org/new_york_index.html

The Minneapolis Institute of Arts
www.artsmia.org

Further Reading

General Art Books

Beckett, Wendy. *The Story of Painting.* New York: Dorling Kindersley Publishing, 2000.

Barber, Nicola, and Mary Moore. *The World of Art.* New York: Silver Burdett Press, 1998.

Brommer, Gerald F. *Discovering Art History.* Worcester, Mass.: Davis Publications, Inc., 1997.

Brommer, Gerald F. and Nancy Kline. *Exploring Painting.* Worcester, Mass.: Davis Publications, Inc., 1995.

Cumming, Robert. *Annotated Guides: Art.* New York: Dorling Kindersley Publishing, 1995.

Curatorial Staff of the Metropolitan Museum of Art. *The Metropolitan Museum of Art Guide.* New York: The Metropolitan Museum of Art, 1994.

Greenaway, Shirley. *Art: An A-Z Guide.* Danbury, Conn.: Franklin Watts, 2000.

Grovignon, Brigette. *The Beginner's Guide to Art.* New York: Harry N. Abrams, Inc., 1998.

Grolier Editorial Staff. *Looking at Art.* Danbury, Conn.: Grolier Educational Books, Inc., 1996.

Hollingsworth, Patricia. *Smart Art: Learning to Classify and Critique Art.* Tucson, Ariz.: Zephyr Press, 1998.

Mallory, Nancy. *European Art Since 1850.* New York: Facts on File Publishing, 1997.

Books about Expressionist Artists

Beckmann

Bezzola, Tobia. *Max Beckmann and Paris: The Exhibition Catalog.* New York: Taschen America LLC, 1998. This book includes illustrations of Beckmann's art.

Gohr, Seigfreid. *Max Beckmann: Paintings, Drawings, Works on Paper.* New York: Michael Werner, Inc., 1994. This book includes illustrations of Beckmann's art.

Kandinsky

Dabrowski, Magdalena. *Kandinsky: Compositions.* New York: The Museum of Modern Art, 1995. This book contains illustrations of Kandinsky's art.

Kandinsky, Wassily. *Kandinsky.* New York: Dorling Kindersley Publishing, 1999.

Klee

Chelsea House Publishing Staff. *Paul Klee.* Broomall, Penn.: Chelsea House, 1997.

Kollwitz

Kollwitz, Käthe. *The Drawings of Kollwitz.* Los Angeles: Borden Publishing, 2000.

Munch

Bischoff, Ulrich. *Munch.* New York: Taschen America LLC, 1996.

Eggum, Arne, and Gerd Woll. *Munch at the Munch Museum, Oslo.* New York: Scala Books, 1998.

Schiele

Fischer, Wolfgang. *Egon Schiele.* New York: Taschen America LLC, 1998.

Kallir, Jane. *Egon Schiele: The Complete Works.* New York: Harry N. Abrams, 1998. This book contains illustrations of Schiele's art.

Index